TARGET TONES

How to Target the right notes, at the right time, all the time over chords and progressions

by David Brewster

To access audio visit:
www.halleonard.com/mylibrary

Enter Code
5064-3308-6677-8224

ISBN 978-1-57424-350-5
SAN 683-8022

Cover by James Creative Group

Photo of David Brewster by Courtney Simon

David Brewster is an honors graduate from the Atlanta Institute of Music, and has several books published by Hal Leonard, Centerstream Publications, and Cherry Lane. He's also a writer and contributor for Guitar Player and Premier Guitar magazine.

In addition to his educational background and published works, he's taught guitar and music for over 20 years, including teaching for Guitar Center Studios, The National Guitar Workshop, School of Rock, and at colleges and universities across the Midwest.

His performance background includes touring and recording with several national acts, and David has independently released several instrumental guitar albums, including music tributes to Edgar Allan Poe, HR Giger, and HP Lovecraft.

For more information about David, visit his Soundcloud profile at www.soundcloud.com/david-brewster

Special thanks go to Courtney Simon, who helped me edit and save this book! We're soulmates and you've stolen my heart. Thanks babe! XOXO

Table of Contents

Introduction...4

Chapter 1 –

An Introduction To Targeting 5

Targeting in Rock Music...6

15 Targeted Classic Rock Guitar Solos 7

Melodic Development And Construction 8

The Use Of Looping/Recording In This Book 9

Chapter 2 –

Targeting Minor Chords And Progressions...10

Targeted Approaches In A Minor 12

Targeting The Minor 3rd 15

Chapter 3 –

Targeting Major Chords And Progressions 19

Targeted Approaches In C Major...21

Chapter 4 –

Targeting Hybrid Pentatonic Scales 27

Targeting The Major 3rd..29

Chapter 5 –

Targeting The Natural Minor Scale 34

Chapter 6 –

Intervals And "The Pentatonic Highway" 41

The Pentatonic Highway..43

Chapter 7 –

A Brief History Of Looping In Music 47

Introduction

Welcome to Target Tones!

This strategic soloing guide will help any guitarist understand how to play over chords and chord progressions intelligently, which will help any player learn how to target the right notes, at the right time, all the time.

Targeting specific notes from a scale over a chord is the basic concept behind this method, and learning how to target certain notes over chords and progressions will improve your improvisational skills significantly. It will also improve your overall awareness of how you can arrange and organize what you're playing during a riff, fill, or solo.

The concepts shared in this method will reveal some of the mystery of what happens when scales are played over chords and progressions. This area of study can take a lifetime of refinement and discovery, and expressing yourself fully using a musical instrument is the ultimate goal for any musician.

In time, your ability to be able to play what you hear in your head will become a reality, and studying the fundamentals of chord-scale relationships will greatly improve your soloing skills and overall awareness of music in a short amount of time. As you begin targeting notes over chords and progressions, your lead lines and phrases will begin sounding cohesive, interesting, and musical.

One of the key components of this method is the inclusion of loop-based technology as these concepts and sounds are introduced and revealed. The ability of looping, recording, or sustaining the individual chords and chord progressions behind you as you experiment with these concepts is crucial. This type of aural practice will fully define what you're learning as you progress, and will help you absorb these concepts and ideas instantly.

As you begin using a targeted soloing approach, your ability to connect melodically with the chords and progressions you're playing over will improve dramatically. In time, you'll increase your awareness of playing over various chords and progressions and improve your overall musicianship of understanding how chords and scales function and work together.

Be sure to take your time and be creative and open-minded to new ideas and concepts as you work through this material. It was written to help you become an aware soloist in a short amount of time, and leaves plenty of room for musical improvisation and experimentation using your own ideas.

Good luck!

Chapter 1 – *An Introduction to Targeting*

The premise behind this book is simple - learning how to target specific notes over individual chords and chord progressions.

In the beginning, you'll target the strongest and safest note choice possible - the root. It doesn't matter what key, chord, or chord progression you're playing over if you target the root of the chord, it will always sound good.

Emphasizing and targeting the root is the first area to develop, and as you become comfortable targeting the root, you can begin targeting other chord tones and notes specific to the key, chord type, or progression. This includes strong note choices - such as the 3rd and 5th. These additional targeted notes will add a level of variance to your licks and phrases and will offset the sound of always beginning or ending your phrases on the root.

The concept of targeting chord tones is a great way to build cohesive and melodic sounds in your music. You can easily find targeted phrasing and soloing in every style of music. It's especially common in blues, rock, metal, country, and jazz music, and you can find countless guitarists using some form of this melodic soloing approach.

Targeting notes while playing is a simple concept and involves emphasizing or accenting the note(s) selected, usually accompanied using a rhythmic or melodic hook. In musical terms and related to specific techniques for the guitar, this is normally accomplished using expressive string-bending, emphasized vibrato phrasing, strong rhythms and accents, and using a series of targeted melodic ideas to create a memorable solo.

There are several soloing approaches that you can use, but for our purposes in this method, we're discovering and exploring two types of targeted melodic approaches, which are known as *key-center* and *chord-tone* soloing.

Key-Center Soloing - involves finding the tonal center of what you're playing over and identifying a single scale that will fit over the entire progression or solo section.
This soloing approach is very common in blues and blues-influenced music, including rock, country, jazz, funk, and many other musical styles. This one scale approach can be found almost everywhere in guitar music, and while it's a viable option, it commonly leaves the listener and soloist wanting more. This partially explains why many players using a key-center approach will include outside notes or chromatic passing tones to their licks, phrases, and solos.

Chord-Tone Soloing - involves finding the scales and modes that connect over each chord, and will help you strategically move through the chord progression.
This soloing approach is very common in jazz, rock, metal, bluegrass, and classical music, and creates a stronger connection with the chord progression you're playing over. While it takes more effort and thought to navigate through a chord progression using this approach, the phrases, sounds, melodies, and ideas you'll create when using this concept are worth the extra effort and study.

This book is written around a small collection of guitar-friendly keys, and every guitarist should find themselves playing or performing in (at least) one of them. These keys include *A Minor*, *C Major*, *G Major*, and *E Minor*. Once you've worked through these popular and common keys in this book, you can apply the Target Tones approach to other keys, tonalities, chords, and chord progressions.

As you begin working with these concepts and dive into this method, keep this in mind – no matter what key or chord you're playing over, the root of the chord will always sound good, as long as you're in tune. Once you understand how to target and use the root note in your licks and phrases, then you can begin to sample and explore other note options, which will create and yield plenty of new and interesting ideas.

Targeting in Rock Music

Historically, guitarists in all styles of music have utilized a targeted soloing approach, and while the bulk of this revolves around a blues-influenced soloing style, the targeted concepts and approaches shown in this method can be applied to any style of music. It's highly recommended to expand these ideas into as many styles, areas, and places as possible. The more you learn - the more there is to learn.

The list of guitarists who pioneered targeted soloing approaches is lengthy, and the best place to begin is a serious study of blues music and the ideas contained therein. Blues music eventually gave birth to rock, country, jazz, funk, folk, and a wide-range of musical styles, and there's plenty you can learn from studying the music and phrasing of blues guitar legends, with players such as B.B. King, Albert King, and John Lee Hooker - to name a few.

To origin of targeting in rock guitar music began in the mid-1950's, and can be traced back to the birth of the rock genre. The king of the early days is guitar legend Chuck Berry, who single-handedly paved the way for legions of rock guitarists that followed in his footsteps. Other popular and notable pickers around this time include Carl Perkins, Scotty Moore, and Link Wray, each of whom further shaped the role of the electric guitar in the flourishing and booming style of rock and roll.

As rock music entered the 1960's, there were several important guitarists that pushed melodic guitar playing and targeted soloing further, while rock music continued to evolve, change, and mutate. The new breed of rock guitarist in the 1960's reached for plenty of blues-based ideas and phrases, not to mention a number of standard Major and Minor scales and ideas. This decade also contained plenty of exotic scales and unique modal flavors, with guitarists such as George Harrison, Robby Kreiger, and Keith Richards leading the charge into targeted and melodic rock music bliss.

By the end of the 1960's, rock guitarists and music fans were captivated by a group of British blues-rock heroes, including Eric Clapton, Jimmy Page, Jeff Beck, Pete Townshend, and Peter Green. Another notable melodic marvel named Carlos Santana was musically flourishing during this period and delivered several inspired albums and performances as the 1960's moved into the 1970's.

Rock guitar pioneer Chuck Berry posing in his famous "duck walk" in the 1950's.

Jimi Hendrix has been named one of the greatest guitarists of all-time and he thrived during this time. Hendrix directly influenced and inspired all of the guitarists from England mentioned above during the 1960's, not to mention the

millions his music has inspired over the years. His signature blues-influenced rock guitar style and sound has become the bar that many guitarists use to measure themselves, musically speaking.

Enter the 1970's and melodic targeted guitar playing can be found in full swing, with a number of influential guitar heroes leading the way. This decade reveals melodic masters such as Jeff Beck, Jimmy Page, David Gilmour, Joe Walsh, and Billy Gibbons. Each of these players helped to develop melodic note-targeting further and introduced new audiences to their own manner of blues-influenced rock guitar playing.

Guitar legend Jimi Hendrix live in the late 1960's. One of the greatest electric guitarists of all-time.

By the end of the 1970's, a young punk from California named Eddie Van Halen turned the rock guitar world upside-down. While his flash and flurries of notes are dizzying to comprehend, Van Halen always has a knack for bringing memorable melodic phrases out in his licks, fills, and solos.

Once the 1980's had arrived, rock guitarists found themselves pushing their technique further than ever. Aside from the large group of shred guitar heroes that exploded onto the scene, led by frontrunners such as Yngwie Malmsteen, Paul Gilbert, Joe Satriani, and Steve Vai, the technical prowess of these players cannot be ignored, and neither can their focus of building melodically-minded music performed at hyperactive and dizzying speeds.

Guitar genius Jeff Beck first became popular in the 1960's, and continues to push his music to this day.

The 1990's continued to spawn new players onto the rock scene, and each of them is noteworthy and influential for pushing melodic guitar playing and music even further. This decade included grunge and alternative legends such as Jerry Cantrell, Adam Jones, Buckethead, and Tom Morello, to name a few. The grunge and alternative movement during this decade helped usher in a new direction and flavor for rock guitarists to explore, which was created using a loose, raw, and "rough-around-the-edges" musical approach.

As new music in the 21st Century continues to spawn new sounds, textures, ideas, and directions for guitarists to explore, the future will continually create new generations of musicians, each pushing their music into new areas, sounds, and directions. This includes the unique sounds and ideas heard coming from players such as Tosin Abasi, Pilini, and Jeff Loomis.

15 Targeted Classic Rock Guitar Solos

One of the best ways to improve your awareness of how to create and play targeted melodic phrases and licks would be to examine and analyze the work from some of your favorite guitarists. Pick a song and a solo, and then begin your analysis.

It would be wise to start with locating an accurate transcription of the song or solo you're going to tackle, which will be your road map and uncover exactly what was played. The transcription will also reveal clues to the most important mystery behind *why* they played what they played, and how you can gain access to this realm of musical ability.

Working closely with great music will improve your ability to write your own music and produce the music you hear in your head. To help you get started, the list below features fifteen classic rock songs that feature highly influential guitar licks, fills, and solos. This is a great collection of music to learn from and examine, and you should notice that many of these popular songs are classic rock standards, which are frequently heard in movies, television shows, commercials, and on the radio.

15 Targeted Classic Rock Guitar Solos

1. Chuck Berry - 'Johnny B. Goode' (1958)
2. Jimi Hendrix - 'All Along The Watchtower' (1968)
3. Eric Clapton - 'White Room' (1968)
4. Carlos Santana - 'Black Magic Woman' (1970)
5. Jimmy Page - 'Stairway To Heaven' (1971)
6. Elliot Randall - 'Reelin' In The Years' (1972)
7. Joe Walsh - 'Rocky Mountain Way' (1973)
8. Billy Gibbons - 'La Grange' (1973)
9. Jeff Beck - 'Cause We've Ended As Lovers' (1975)
10. Brian May - 'Bohemian Rhapsody' (1975)
11. Tom Scholz - 'More Than A Feeling' (1976)
12. Joe Walsh & Don Felder - 'Hotel California' (1976)
13. Neal Schon - 'Lights' (1978)
14. Mark Knopfler - 'Sultans Of Swing' (1979)
15. David Gilmour - 'Comfortably Numb' (1979)

Legends of the guitar - Jimi Hendrix, Eric Clapton, Jimmy Page, and Jeff Beck have created a sonic blueprint that you can use as a soloing template, which will help you understand how to begin creating your own licks and ideas. All of the songs listed above will serve as a great point of reference, helping you to hear some of the greatest guitar solos ever recorded. Each of these songs is a historic example of targeted musical magic, and needless to say - you can learn a lot from studying the music of the legends within any style or musical genre.

Melodic Development And Construction

As you move forward and begin targeting over chords, it's highly suggested to build a solid foundation of melodic construction and developmental techniques. As you'll discover, there are many ways to approach playing melodically over chords, and it's highly suggested to experiment with as many melodic techniques and approaches as possible.

The list below reveals ten of the strongest components of building strong melodies and melodic material in your music. This is the general basis for building licks and phrases and will eventually be combined to build guitar solos.

10 Useful Melodic Techniques

1. Passing Tones
2. Escape Tones
3. Neighbor Tones
4. Changing Tones
5. Pedal-Point Phrasing
6. Melodic Anticipation
7. Melodic Suspension
8. Melodic Embellishment
9. Melodic Arpeggiation
10. Melodic/Rhythmic Variation

The melodic techniques listed above will be incorporated and scattered throughout this book. It's highly recommended to learn as much as you can about intervals, scale construction, chord construction, chord progressions, melodic phrasing, and more. These concepts and areas of music theory are the essential components of creating memorable and melodic music.

While becoming aware of the various melodic approaches and techniques available to you as a soloist, you'll gain access to the same ideas and approaches your favorite guitarists use when they play. Historically, there are numerous melodic guitar pioneers, including fretboard legends such as Django Reinhardt, Charlie Christian, Wes Montgomery, B.B. King, James Burton, Chet Atkins, and many other masters of melody. These players helped redefine the guitar for the modern age, and introduced several techniques and approaches of performing melodically on the guitar.

As this book progresses, you'll learn more about these melodic techniques and approaches listed above, and you'll find that most of these approaches and techniques are very common in a variety of musical styles. When you're working with melodic construction, any time you find something that you like, be sure to spend additional time focusing on these areas that peak your interest or perk your ears.

The Use Of Looping/Recording In This Book

This instructional method uses loop technology throughout and being able to have the chords and progressions sound behind you as you play through these licks, phrases, and ideas will give you the full experience and benefit of working with this book. If you're unable to obtain or acquire a loop pedal, you can use a general recording device, a voice/sound recorder from a cell phone or computer, or the assistance of another musician to provide to necessary chords and backing that you'll need, which will help you hear what you're targeting and playing.

Having someone play these chords and progressions behind you is highly recommended, and is a great way to actually *hear* this material and what you're playing. Playing along with other musicians while using this targeted approach should be one of your goals, in addition to gaining a stronger insight with using targeted soloing concepts and strategies.

The convenient thing about using a loop pedal as you practice and rehearse this material is it gives you the opportunity to make mistakes and work through the uncertainty of what you're practicing and learning at your own pace. This type of practice can give you chance to get a grip on using scales, improvisation, and other soloing concepts in private, and eventually, you can reveal what you've learned while playing or jamming with other musicians.

As you work from this method, you'll notice the combination of visual cues shown below attached to each example. These two symbols are instructions that direct when to loop/sustain an individual chord or progression, and when to play the various licks, phrases, and ideas that you'll be learning.

LOOP

The "Loop" graphic highlights what is to be looped or recorded.

PLAY

The "Play" graphic highlights what is to be played over the looped backing.

As you improvise and play over looped backing tracks, take additional time playing and creating your own licks, ideas, and phrases. In time, you'll become more comfortable creating your own looped backing tracks to jam and solo over.

You can eventually create challenging or more complicated backing rhythms, riffs, chord progressions, and move into other keys, but it's always a good idea to start slow and explore the basics first. From there, you can always up the ante and move into more complicated progressions, modal keys, and various other directions.

To get the full experience of working from this book, (once again) it's highly recommended to use a loop pedal, recorder, or sampling device to deliver the sound the individual chords or chord progressions that you'll be playing over. This will help you clearly understand how to use a targeted approach as you solo and how to interact with various chords and progressions.

Chapter 2 – *Targeting Minor Chords And Progressions*

To begin targeting over Minor chords and progressions, let's begin with the most obvious note choice - the root. The root of the chord is the most stable and transparent note that you can perform, and this note will always sound good to the ear. Once you've become comfortable targeting the root, you can begin targeting other chord tones or notes from the key.

The next diagram reveals the breakdown of the A Minor Pentatonic scale and what you're actually producing when you play this common scale over an A Minor chord. Notice the intervallic spelling and terminology used in this diagram. The construction and arrangement of intervals are *very* important to learn, but for now, move forward and become familiar with these basic names, terms, and sounds.

Breakdown Of A Minor Pentatonic

A - C - D - E - G - (A)
1 - b3 - 4 - 5 - b7 - (1)

A - *The root. The strongest and safest targeted note.*

C - *The Minor 3rd. A stable interval that wants to resolve to the root or the 5th.*

D - *The Perfect 4th. A stable interval that wants to resolve to the root or the 5th.*

E - *The Perfect 5th. A stable interval that wants to resolve to the root.*

G - *The Minor 7th. An unstable interval that wants to resolve to the root or the 5th.*

A - *The Octave. A stable and transparent interval used in all styles of music.*

The first example is a basic demonstration of performing the A Minor Pentatonic scale over the A Minor chord. As you play **Ex.1**, pay attention to how each note of the scale sounds as it's played against the chord. To broaden the sound, feel free to add vibrato to any of these notes as you play through the scale, which will give this scale a realistic flavor as you play over the chord.

Ex. 1

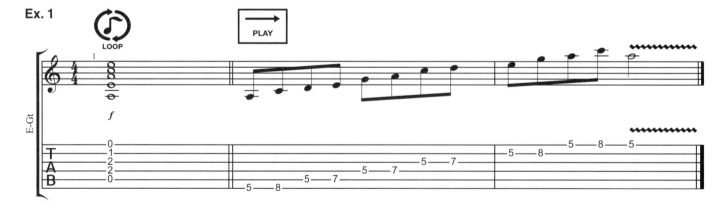

For a better view of where the root is located within the A Minor Pentatonic scale, **Ex.2** reveals where to find the root note 'A' within this common "box" scale fingering. Notice that you can access the root by bending the 8th fret of the 'B' string up a whole step, raising the note 'G' to the root 'A.'

Ex. 2

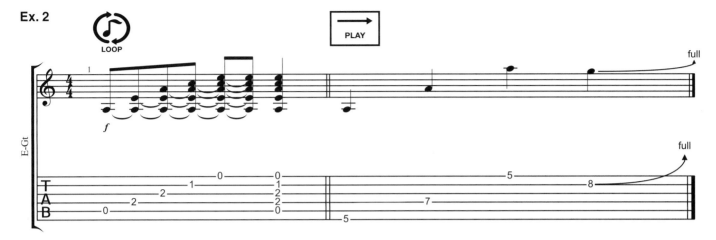

Once you see where the root is located, listen to how the scale is affected when played over the A Minor chord. The following diagram will give you visual insight into what you're hearing as you play the A Minor Pentatonic scale against the matching chord. Notice the melodic and harmonic attraction the notes of the scale have against the chord as they're performed.

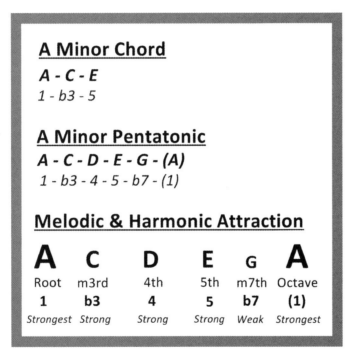

In the diagram above, the *Melodic & Harmonic Attraction* area at the bottom lists the individual notes of the scale, but they're written and sized according to the relationship and strength they have when they're played against the A Minor chord. As you can see, the note 'A' is the strongest, the 3rd (C), 4th (D), and 5th (E) are stable chord tones, while the 7th (G) is weaker and wants to resolve to a stronger note after it's targeted or performed.

Targeted Approaches In A Minor

The first targeted concept you should tackle includes the process of approaching the note 'A' from above and below. As you play through each of these variations, notice how each new phrase has a different sound and that these simple variations can lead your fingers toward plenty of original phrases and licks. **Ex.3** will help you get things started, targeting the root 'A' from one note below and one note above.

Ex. 3

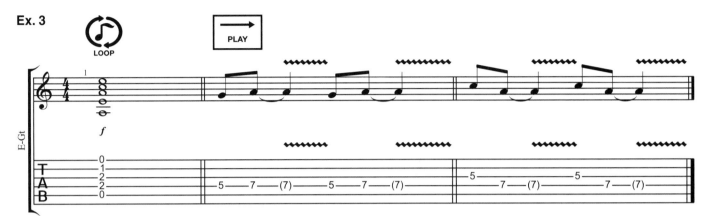

Ex.4 approaches the targeted root from two notes below and above, by adding one note to the previous example.

Ex. 4

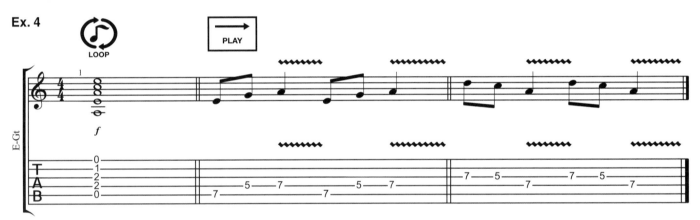

Moving to **Ex.5**, you'll see that we're approaching from three notes below and above the root. Continue creating your own variations of these approaches and lick-building phrases.

Ex. 5

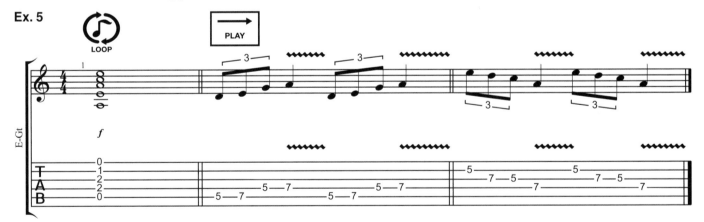

Ex.6 moves this concept into a four-note approach from below and above. Notice how we're mutating this simple scale exercise into the creation of authentic-sounding licks and phrases.

Ex. 6

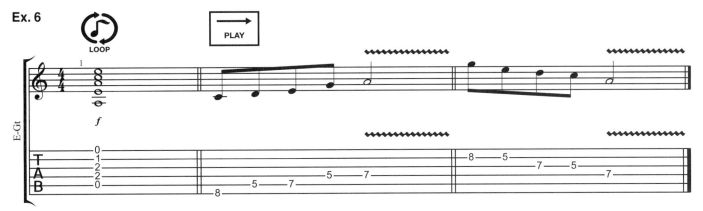

As you're becoming comfortable targeting the root using different note groupings and approaches, you can begin playing and creating various combination licks and phrases, similar to the targeted combinations found in **Ex.7**

Ex. 7

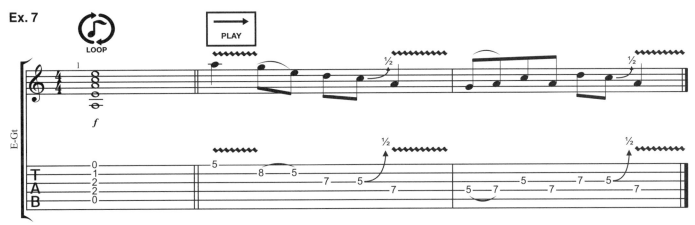

For a more developed example of how you can combine different note groupings melodically, **Ex.8** reveals a short targeted phrase that you can use as a template to help you build additional licks and phrases.

Ex. 8

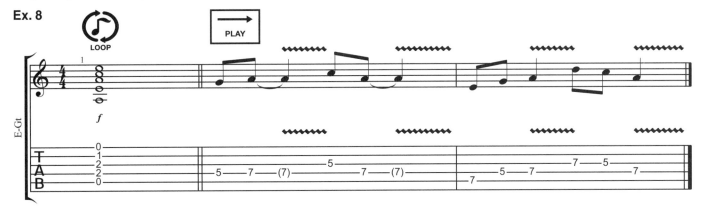

Once you're comfortable targeting the root using different approaches over the A Minor chord, let's expand this idea to target the root of the next chord we'll add to the chord progression, which is the iv chord of this key - D Minor.

The second half of **Ex.9** reveals where you can locate the root note 'D,' and you should practice targeting this note over the looped D Minor chord in the first bar. Be aware that 'D' can also be reached by bending the 8th fret of the high E string, strategically raising the note 'C' a whole-step up to 'D.'

Ex. 9

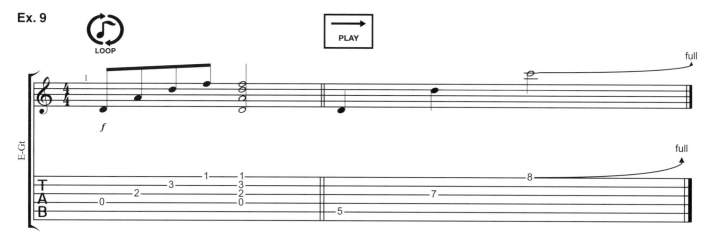

Ex.10 contains a looped two-chord progression, and the lead part features an example of how you can target the root of both of these chords within this short two-bar demonstration.

Ex. 10

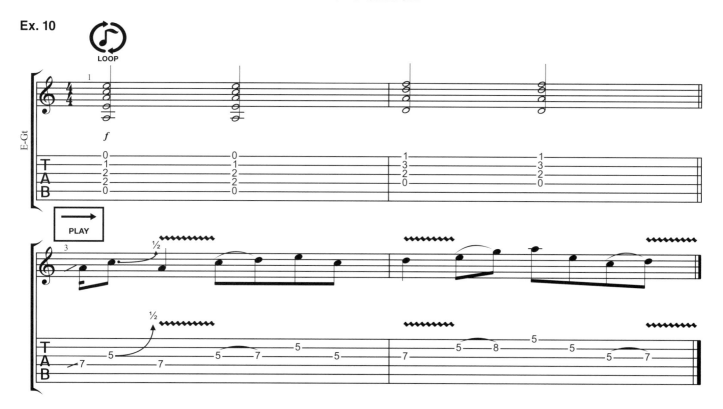

Spend some additional time improvising over this two-chord progression before moving ahead. Be sure you have a grasp on targeting the root notes as this progression moves from chord-to-chord. Pay attention to what you're playing and what chords you're playing over, and you'll begin to improve your soloing skills and melodic awareness immediately.

Targeting The Minor 3rd

Instead of always targeting the root of the chord, you can begin targeting additional notes over the chord, which will yield plenty of new and interesting sounds. Another solid note that you should target in your licks and phrases is the powerful and expressive sound of the 3rd.

Ex.11 targets the note 'C' in the first bar, which is an appropriate Minor 3rd played against the A Minor chord. The second bar shows how you can target the 'F' note on 6th fret of the B string. This is the Minor 3rd of D Minor and sounds great matched against the chord ringing in the background.

Ex. 11

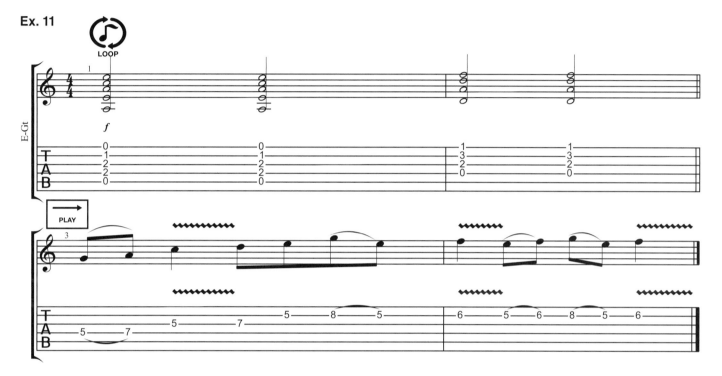

It might take a while to become comfortable targeting notes other than the root, but in time your skill of using additional target tones will improve, and your solos and phrases will move into exciting new directions.

The next example features a targeted four-bar solo and will lead your fingers toward several interesting directions. **Ex.12** displays how to create a balance between targeting the root and the Minor 3rd, which will help your phrases sound more authentic and musical.

Ex. 12

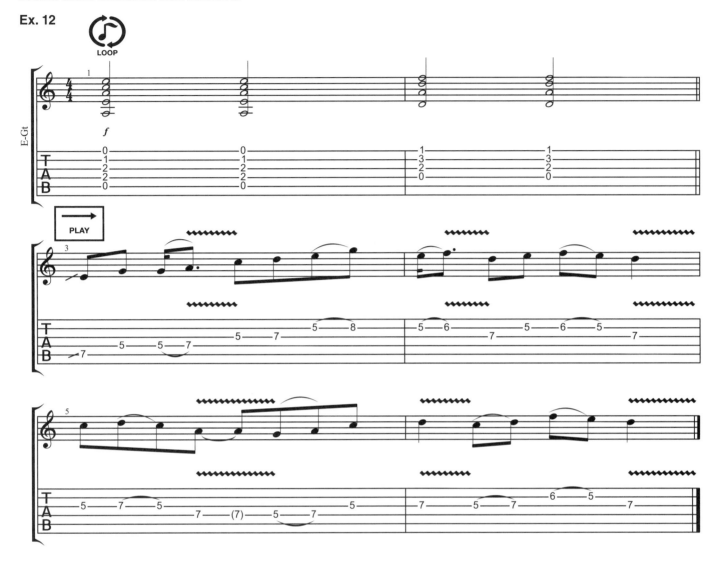

The goal here is to become comfortable targeting the root and third between the A Minor and D Minor chords as this chord progression occurs. The next section in this chapter will expand this chord progression and these concepts further.

The next chord we'll include is the last piece of the puzzle - the E Minor chord. The inclusion of this chord will transform what we've already played into a full i-iv-v progression. In the key of A Minor, these chords are A Minor (i), D Minor (iv), and E Minor (v).

Ex.13 reveals and targets the root notes over the next chord we're adding - E Minor.

Ex. 13

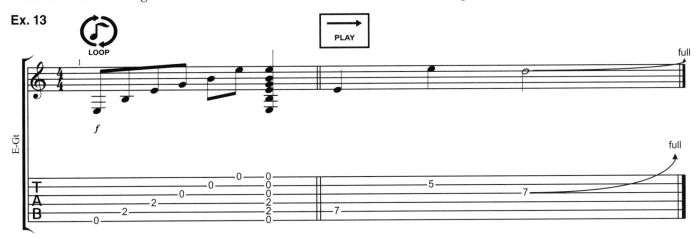

Now that you have the root notes for each of these chords mapped out and comfortable under your fingers, you're ready to tackle navigating through the Am-Dm-Em chord progression. A basic targeted sample approach is shown in **Ex.14**.

Ex. 14

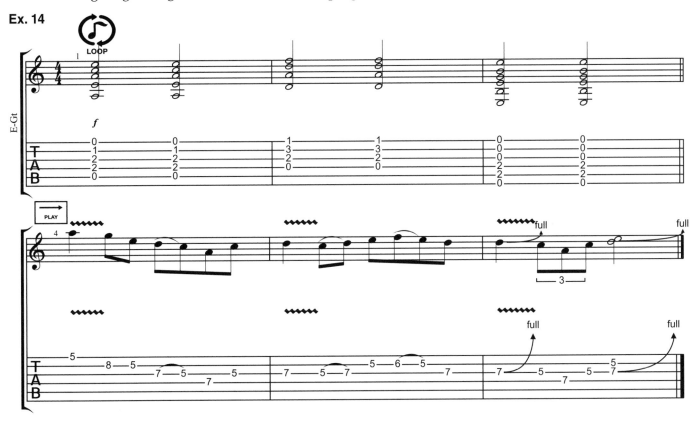

Be sure to take your time playing over this three chord progression, and build upon these movements, concepts, and ideas, especially as this book moves into other keys, scales, and tonalities.

The final example in this chapter demonstrates a four-bar targeted solo over the i-iv-v progression in A Minor. This will give you a solid template to begin building your own ideas and phrases over this common progression. As you can see, **Ex.15** features plenty of interesting targeted movements and ideas for you to discover and borrow.

Ex. 15

Chapter 3 – *Targeting Major Chords And Progressions*

The next area that we'll explore uses a targeted soloing approach over Major chords and progressions. This is a very familiar sound and can be heard in a variety of music styles, including several generations of pop, rock, country, jazz, folk, and acoustic music.

The following diagram will give you the visual breakdown of using C Major Pentatonic, which is arranged like the diagram from the previous chapter, but this time we're playing in a Major key and producing licks, phrases, and melodies using this common and bright-sounding tonality.

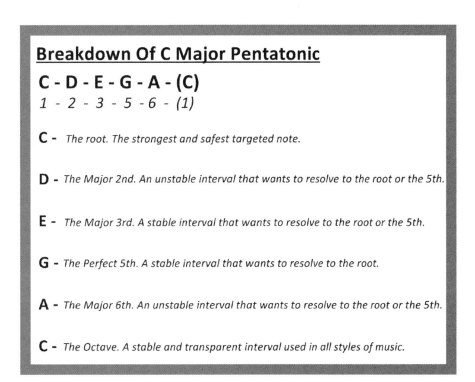

Breakdown Of C Major Pentatonic

C - D - E - G - A - (C)
1 - 2 - 3 - 5 - 6 - (1)

C - *The root. The strongest and safest targeted note.*

D - *The Major 2nd. An unstable interval that wants to resolve to the root or the 5th.*

E - *The Major 3rd. A stable interval that wants to resolve to the root or the 5th.*

G - *The Perfect 5th. A stable interval that wants to resolve to the root.*

A - *The Major 6th. An unstable interval that wants to resolve to the root or the 5th.*

C - *The Octave. A stable and transparent interval used in all styles of music.*

To begin playing over Major chords and keys, **Ex.16** demonstrates how to recycle the exact same scale position and fingering we used to play in the key of A Minor in Chapter 2, but we're using this scale over a C Major chord and tonality, which provides a completely new sound and overall function for this scale.

Ex. 16

As you can see and hear, Ex.16 reveals how this scale can adapt to being played over the C Major chord, by pinpointing and targeting the appropriate chord tones to function and sound properly, which matches the sound of C Major perfectly.

Ex.17 shows where you can find and access the root note 'C' from this Major Pentatonic scale fingering, and this includes the addition of the root found at the 3rd fret on the 'A' string.

Ex. 17

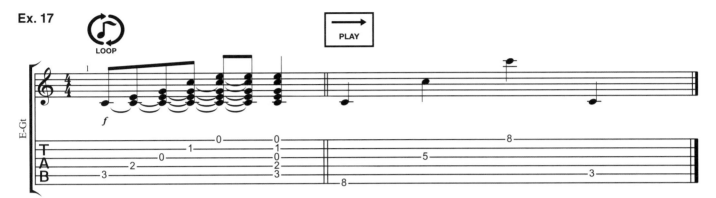

The addition of the root at the 3rd fret is technically out of position compared to where the other root notes are located, but accessing this note from this fretboard location is very popular, and was mainly included to direct your fingers toward expanding your phrases and ideas outside of the basic "box" scale fingering. The notes from this common scale can be relocated and found all over the fretboard, and it's up to you to become aware of where the notes you're searching for are located all over the neck.

The next diagram will give you a visualization similar to what was shared in the previous chapter, but focusing on Major keys and scales. Using this chart as a guide, learn the difference of using this scale over Major chords and progressions.

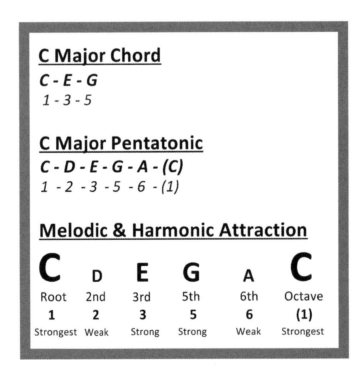

Targeted Approaches In C Major

The next example begins the process of what was explored and shown in the first chapter, as **Ex.18** demonstrates the approach of targeting the root 'C' from one note below and above.

Ex. 18

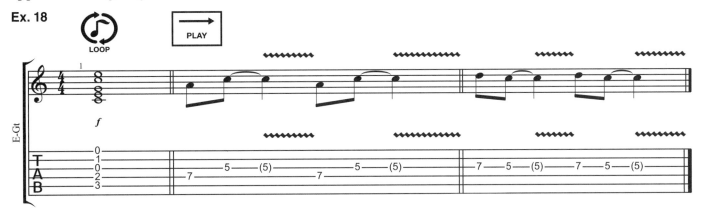

Continue this process with **Ex.19**, featuring a two-note targeted approach over C Major.

Ex. 19

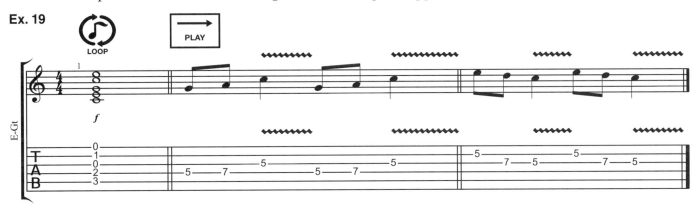

Ex.20 demonstrates how to approach the root from three notes below and above.

Ex. 20

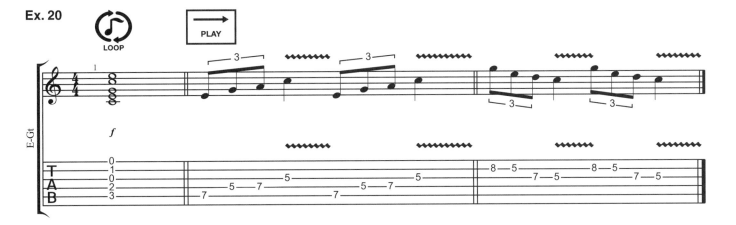

Ex.21 continues this idea by adding a four-note approach from below and above.

Ex. 21

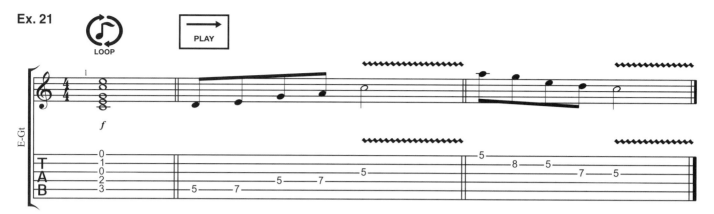

The next example expands this exploration by creating combination licks, and **Ex.22** starts the process of building these types of combined phrases in C Major.

Ex. 22

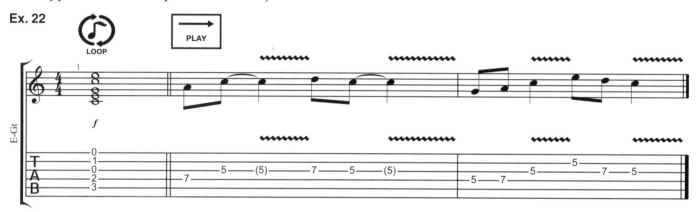

Now that you're comfortable playing and targeting the C Major root, let's add an additional chord to the progression to create a very common progression - the I-IV featuring C and F Major.

If you carefully examine the Major Pentatonic scale structure in this key, you'll notice that it doesn't naturally contain the note 'F,' but we can easily add this note to this scale. **Ex.23** reveals where you can access the note 'F' in this position, including two strategic bending options on the 'A' and 'B' string.

Ex. 23

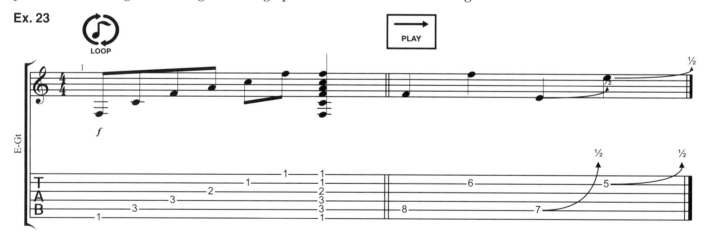

The next example moves to a sample targeted solo, which will help you see how to approach the root notes over this I-IV chord progression. Notice that we're briefly landing on the notes 'E' and 'C' in the first bar of **Ex.24**, but avoiding to sustain or hold anything until we reach the second bar and target on the 'F' root. This type of phrasing can create a sense of movement and interest in your phrases and solos, and you should experiment with creating some additional ideas and licks with this "delayed targeting" concept in mind.

Ex. 24

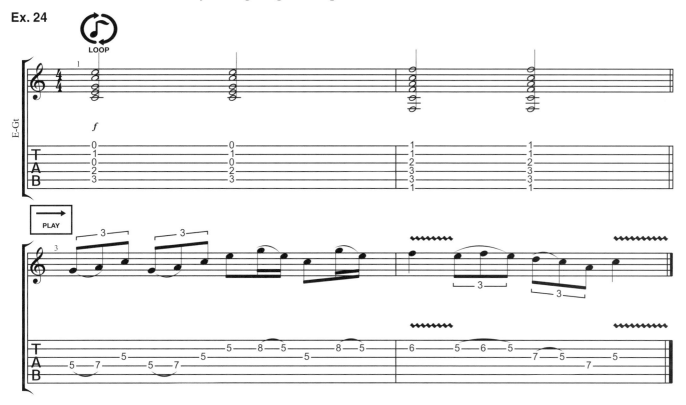

Targeted phasing and movements like this can help you build tension or momentum when you're creating or playing a solo. Take advantage of start-and-stop phrasing like this, and use various targeted note combinations and performance techniques when you're jamming or working on new ideas and material.

Be sure to allow yourself ample time to play and experiment with these ideas, especially when you're tackling new and challenging subjects such as chord/scale relationships, modal playing, intervallic phrasing, and much more. Music can become very complicated rather quickly, and within a few chord moves, a song can shift into an entirely new key or modulate to another tonality in an instant.

As a musician, you should be prepared and aware of *what* you're playing and *why* you're playing it - at all times.

The next example features a four-bar solo to play through, and **Ex.25** will supply you with a few ideas to borrow over this popular chord progression.

Ex. 25

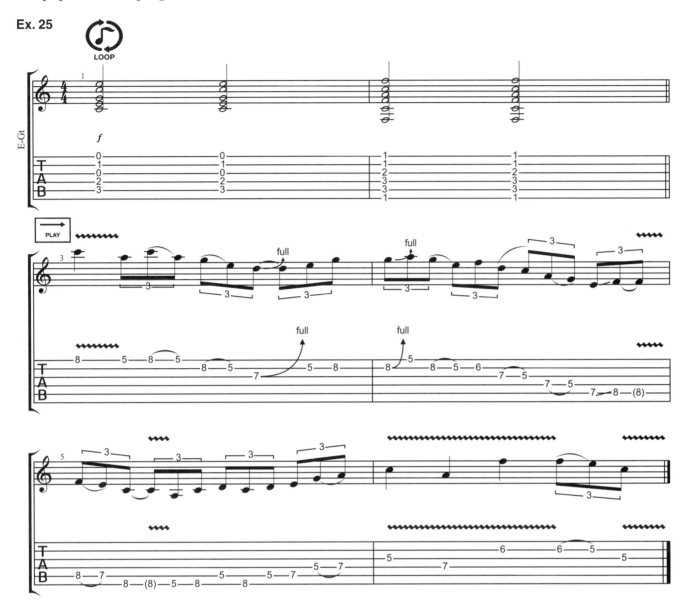

As you continue to jam and play over this progression, strive for creating melodic and musical-sounding phrases. Your ultimate goal should be improvising ideas and phrases that sound musical and melodic, and less like a scale exercise. The addition of various performance techniques will help you create authentic-sounding licks and ideas, and will give your scale-based playing a hefty dose of realism.

Ex.26 reveals where to find the root notes for the next chord we're adding to the progression, G Major. This is the V chord in the key of C, and adding this chord to the progression will create a full I-IV-V progression in C Major.

Ex. 26

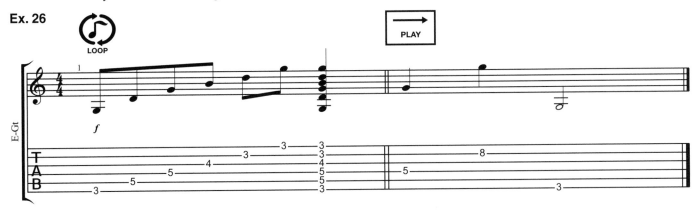

Ex.27 is a sample targeted solo showing you how to approach playing over this common three-chord progression. Notice how the ideas played in the first bar are sustained and build to the busier triplet licks in the second bar, before finally landing on the Major 3rd of 'G' at the beginning of the third bar, and continuing onward with another triplet run at the end.

Ex. 27

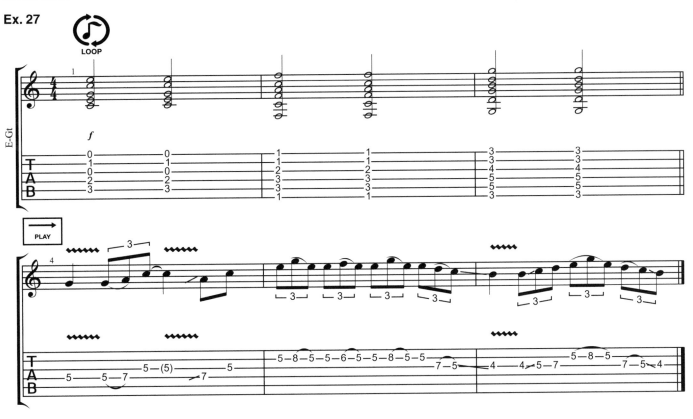

Once you have this three-chord progression playing behind you, you should jam over this chord progression and experiment freely. In time, you'll begin building your own style of licks and phrases over these chords. The ideas that you'll unlock and create of your own design may surprise you.

The final example in this chapter arranges this three-chord progression to build a four-bar solo in C. As you play through **Ex.28**, jam and explore on your own by combining and blending the ideas we've explored in this chapter. In a short amount of time, you'll be able to play and improvise inspired targeted solos effortlessly and spontaneously.

Ex. 28

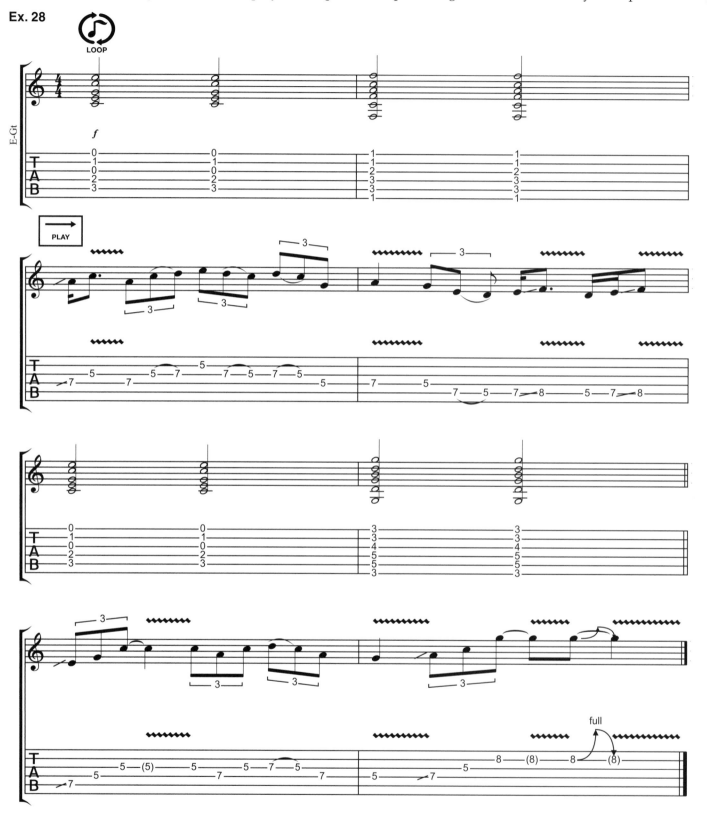

Chapter 4 – *Targeting Hybrid Pentatonic Scales*

This chapter will uncover some of the mystery surrounding playing over Dominant 7th chords and blues-based chord progressions. Hands down, one of the most popular chords progressions on the planet, if not *the* most popular chord progression used in music is the I-IV-V progression.

We've already discussed and used this progression in the previous chapters of this book, but the twist in this chapter is the inclusion of playing a strict combination of Dominant 7th chords. This will give this common I-IV-V progression a slick and blues-based sound and tonality.

The next diagram will reveal the 'hybrid" we'll be using in this chapter, and you should notice the alteration of the structure to the Pentatonic scale, with the inclusion of the Major 3rd to the Minor Pentatonic scale formula. This note is added because we're playing over a G7 chord, which contains this note (B), the appropriate note we're adding to the scale to match over this chord. This additional note will give the Minor Pentatonic scale a Mixolydian modal makeover and an overall Dominant 7th tonality.

Breakdown Of G Hybrid Pentatonic
G - Bb - B - C - D - F - (G)
1 - b3 - 3 - 4 - 5 - b7 - (1)

G - *The root. The strongest and safest targeted note.*

Bb - *The Minor 3rd. An unstable interval that wants to resolve to the root or the 5th.*

B - *The Major 3rd. A stable interval that wants to resolve to the root or the 5th.*

C - *The Perfect 4th. A stable interval that wants to resolve to the root or the 5th.*

D - *The Perfect 5th. A stable interval that wants to resolve to the root.*

F - *The Minor 7th. An unstable interval that wants to resolve to the root or the 5th.*

G - *The Octave. A stable and transparent interval used in all styles of music.*

The Mixolydian scale is one of the most popular modes built from the Major scale, and while we're not going to get into the specifics of modal theory in this book, be aware that the Mixolydian mode fits perfectly over Dominant 7th chords, and is very common in a wide-variety of musical styles.

By adding the Major 3rd to the Minor Pentatonic scale, we're basically flirting with the sound of Mixolydian and altering the scale to match the chord type.

Ex.29 reveals this useful and interesting Mixolydian-flavored "hybrid" Pentatonic alteration.

Ex. 29

The next step is to locate where the root 'G' is located within this fingering and **Ex.30** will guide your fingers to where the root notes are found in this position.

Ex. 30

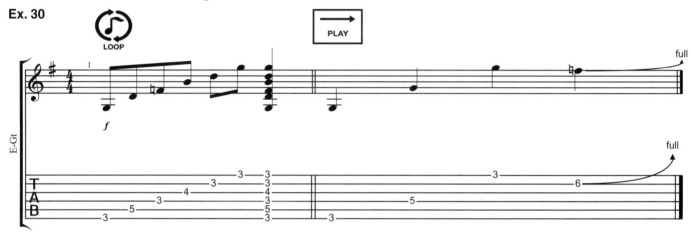

The next diagram examines the overall attraction the notes from this scale have against the chord, similar to what we've analyzed and examined in the previous chapters and areas of this book.

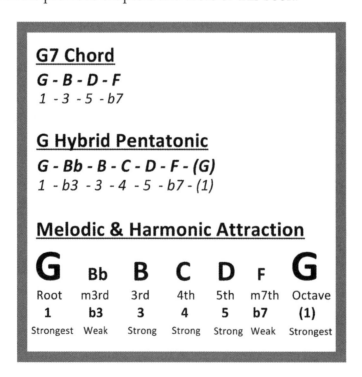

Targeting The Major 3rd

To become acquainted with adding the Major 3rd to the Minor Pentatonic scale, play through the phrases shown in **Ex.31**, which are good examples of how you can approach targeting the Major 3rd in your phrases and ideas.

Ex. 31

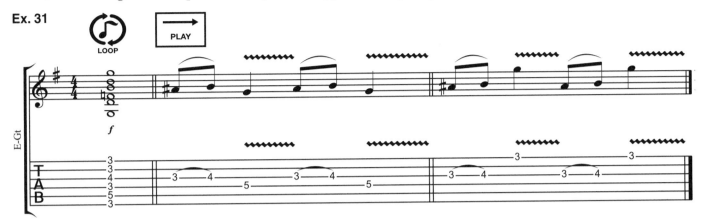

Ex.32 features a lick of using both of the phrases revealed in the previous example, instantly creating a common blues/rock lick.

Ex. 32

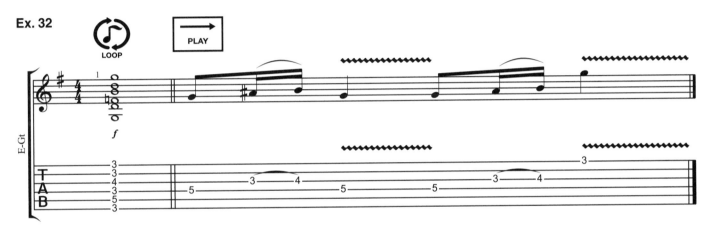

The next example features four developed targeted phrases in the same idea. Notice how **Ex.33** targets the Major 3rd four different ways in this lick.

Ex. 33

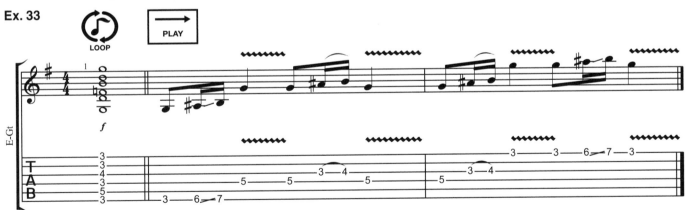

29

Ex.34 introduces where to locate the root notes for the next chord we're adding to the progression - C7. You'll find a number of locations of where you can target 'C,' including the strategic bend on the 6th fret on the high 'E' string.

Ex. 34

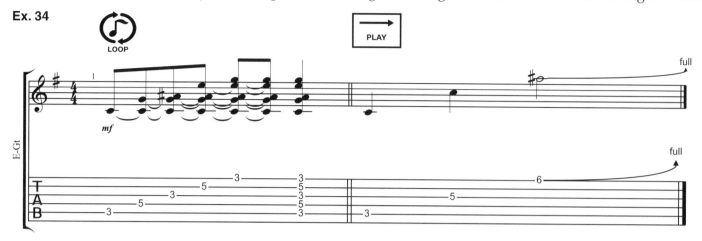

As you become comfortable targeting the Major 3rd over Dominant 7th chord progressions, your blues and rock soloing will drastically improve. Any time you're playing over these bluesy 7th chords, your licks and phrases will sound in-tune and properly matched with the raised Major 3rd, in contrast to the sour sound the Minor 3rd produces against this chord.

Although this tension between the Major and Minor interval can be completely avoided, in blues-rock music the tension created by targeting the Minor 3rd and shifting or bending it to the Major 3rd is very common, and this movement creates a very interesting and familiar sound.

Ex.35 will give you a glimpse of how you can approach soloing over a I7-IV7 progression in G7, and be sure to expand your soloing and ideas further, by continuing to jam and improvise over this popular two-chord progression.

Ex. 35

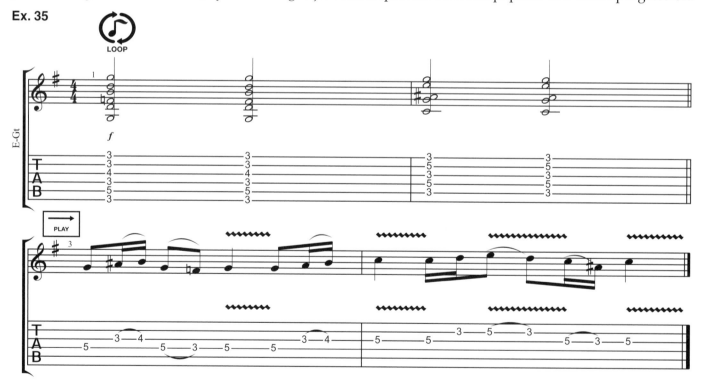

Ex.36 contains a four-bar sample solo over this I-IV progression, which will give you additional insight into blending various Major 3rd targeted ideas overs these two chords. Notice how this example moves freely from one targeted area to the next, as this wandering style of phrasing is common in blues, rock, and jazz music.

Ex. 36

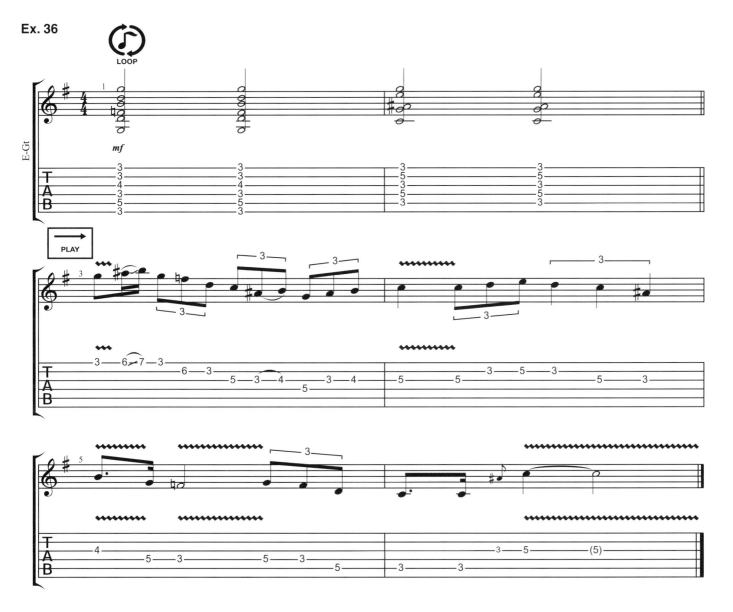

This type of targeted melodic phrasing over chords can be heard in plenty of music from countless guitarists. A few notable melodic masters include Eric Clapton, Billy Gibbons, Eddie Van Halen, Brian May, and Stevie Ray Vaughan, who are each well-known for blazing through chord changes using targeted Pentatonic scales and ideas.

Ex.37 reveals the V chord we're adding to this progression, which includes the famous "Hendrix chord" D7#9. This unusual sounding chord is quite common in rock, blues, funk, jazz, country, and a wide range of other music.

Ex. 37

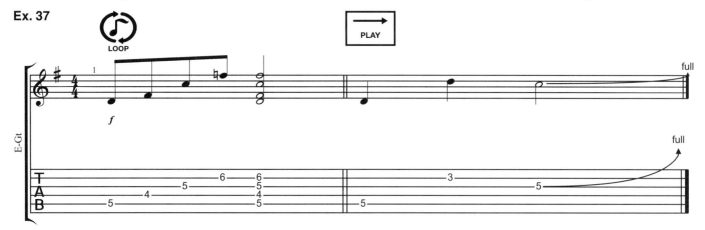

The next example gives you an opportunity to play over this blues progression and **Ex.38** displays the movement between G7 and a new IV chord C9, which helps produce a common blues flavor and sound. The movement to the D7#9 gives this progression a modern twist, very much in the vein of what you'll hear coming from legends such as Jimi Hendrix, Jeff Beck, Robin Trower, and countless others.

Ex. 38

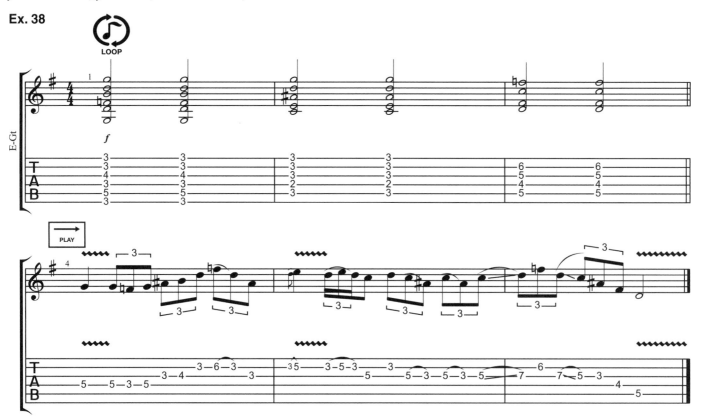

You can hear this type of soloing and movement in the music of plenty of guitar legends, but one of the greatest and most revered is the late blues great Stevie Ray Vaughan. Vaughan is known for playing melodic phrases and bending licks with lots of emotion and feeling, but he was also known for his knuckle-busting licks and busy phrases, which were commonly arranged around a single position or fretboard location.

The final example in this chapter shows an extended four-bar solo to help you become acquainted with properly targeting a full I-IV-V progression in G7. **Ex.39** will show you the way, and you should continue this study by creating your own licks, phrases, and solos based around this common chord progression and tonality.

Ex. 39

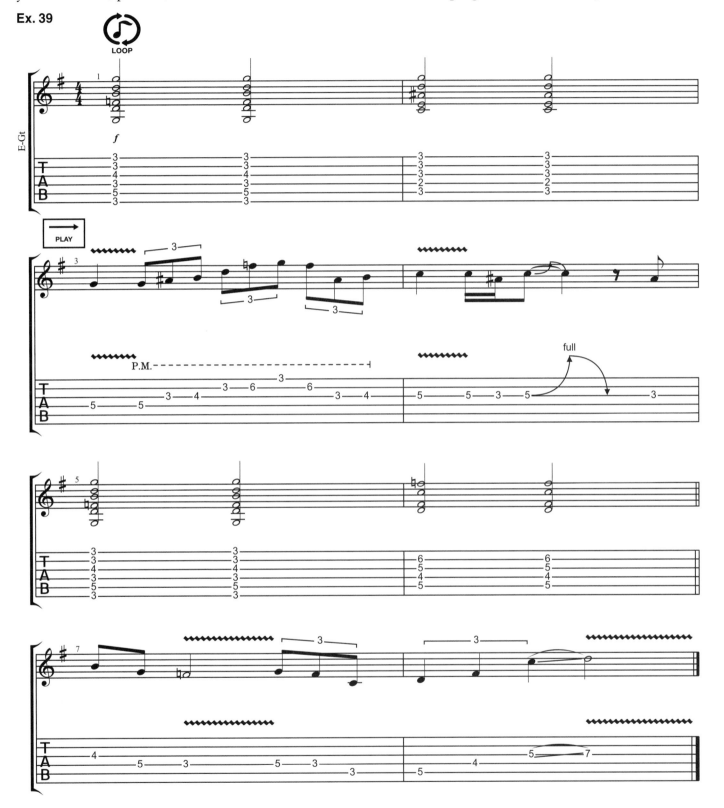

Chapter 5 – *Targeting The Natural Minor Scale*

The next section of this book focuses on how to properly solo using the Natural Minor scale, and the following diagram will give you the basics of getting started using this popular and expressive scale.

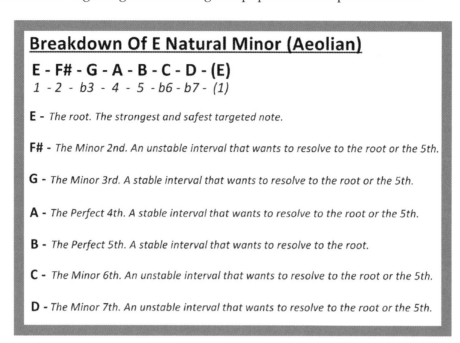

Breakdown Of E Natural Minor (Aeolian)

E - F# - G - A - B - C - D - (E)

1 - 2 - b3 - 4 - 5 - b6 - b7 - (1)

E - *The root. The strongest and safest targeted note.*

F# - *The Minor 2nd. An unstable interval that wants to resolve to the root or the 5th.*

G - *The Minor 3rd. A stable interval that wants to resolve to the root or the 5th.*

A - *The Perfect 4th. A stable interval that wants to resolve to the root or the 5th.*

B - *The Perfect 5th. A stable interval that wants to resolve to the root.*

C - *The Minor 6th. An unstable interval that wants to resolve to the root or the 5th.*

D - *The Minor 7th. An unstable interval that wants to resolve to the root or the 5th.*

Ex.40 will guide your fingers and ears toward using the E Natural Minor Scale.

Ex. 40

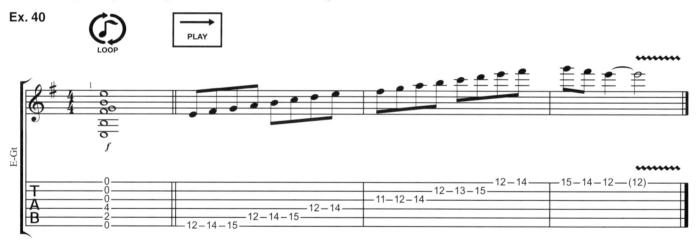

As you become comfortable with this seven-note scale fingering and structure, notice how the additional notes found in this scale gives you additional melodic options, especially when compared to the limited five-note Pentatonic scale structure. You can hear this scale used by countless guitarists in a wide-range of musical styles, including various rock, metal, pop, blues, and jazz players.

Ex.41 exposes where you can find the root notes that will match the interesting sound of the Em9 chord in the first bar. This common chord can be heard in the music of plenty of influential bands, including Pink Floyd and Metallica.

Ex. 41

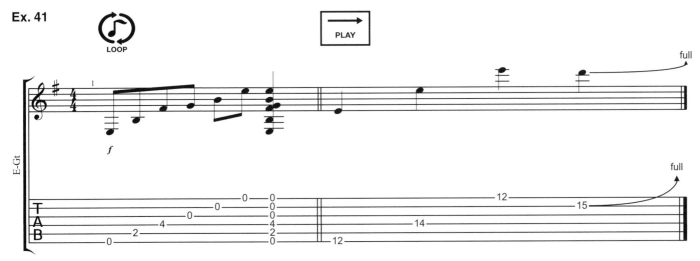

The next diagram will reveal the attraction between the Em9 chord and the E Natural Minor scale.

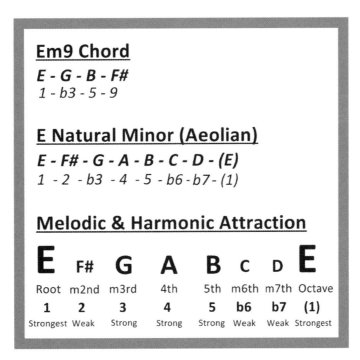

You should notice that the E Natural Minor scale contains all of the notes needed to cover the sound of the Em9 chord, in addition to providing two passing tones, the notes 'A' (the 4th) and 'C' (the 6th) respectively.

The next example will give your fingers and ears a chance to hear how you can target the root and 9th in licks and phrases over this exotic-sounding chord. **Ex.42** is a two-bar melodic phrase that will lead your fingers into the variety of ideas you can locate using the higher positions of the fretboard and this useful scale.

Ex. 42

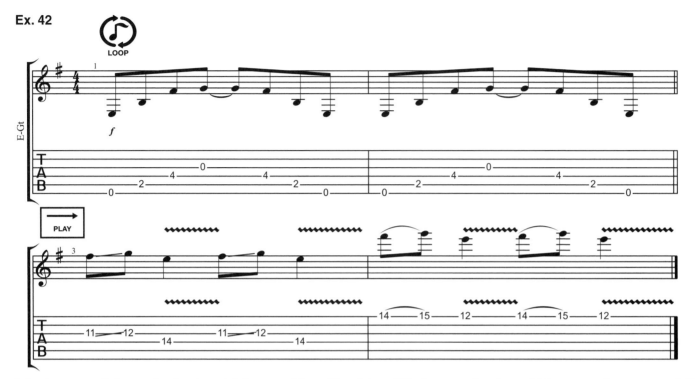

Moving your licks and solos into higher positions like this will help your leads and ideas stand out, especially if you're playing over chord progressions and rhythms that are played in a lower position or octave.

The next idea will move into a busier rock/shred direction, as **Ex.43** features a constant stream of flowing licks and phrases over the Em9 chord.

Ex. 43

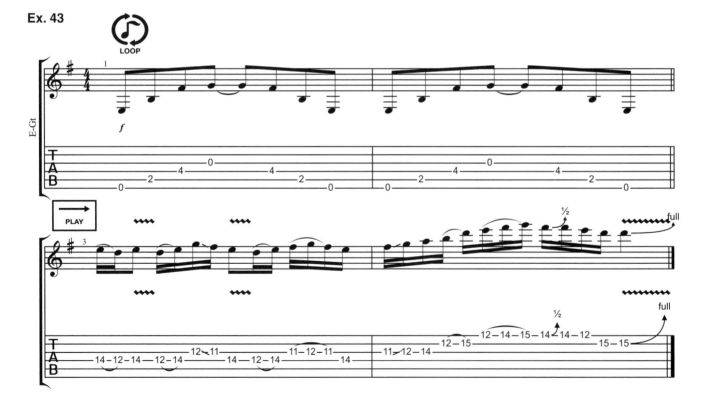

The next example pinpoints where you can find the root of the new chord we're adding to the progression, the very common Am7 chord. **Ex.44** shows where you can locate the roots to target over this chord, including the whole-step bend located at the 15th fret of the high 'E' string, moving the note 'G' up to the root 'A.'

Ex. 44

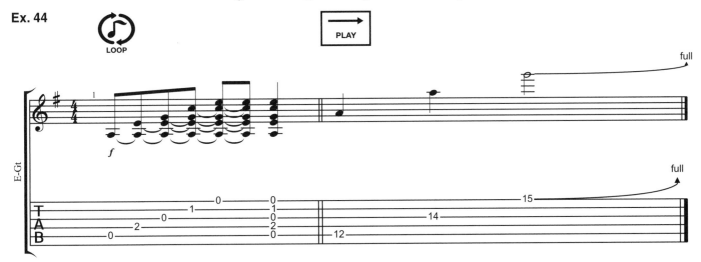

Ex.45 gives you a glimpse into how to target playing over this Em9-Am7 chord progression, while remaining in a modern rock/hard rock style. This busy melodic phrasing has been a staple in a variety of modern rock and metal music, and you can hear these types of licks in the solos of legends such as Steve Morse, Joe Satriani, John Petrucci, and Slash - to name a few.

Ex. 45

As you become comfortable playing and creating licks, phrases, and solos like these in higher positions, seek out some classic solos by some of the previously mentioned guitar legends, and you should also examine music written by your favorite bands and guitarists. Once you unlock some additional licks, phrases, and ideas, try moving what you're learning all over the fretboard and into different keys.

Playing licks and solos using the higher positions of the guitar feels noticeably different compared to the lower positions. The fret spacing, variances in string tension, and the overall position of your hand and wrist while playing can create a range of variables that can affect how and what you find comfortable to play.

The next example displays a four-bar solo to practice, which will help you gain insight into playing over this progression. **Ex.46** reveals a few more ideas to borrow and mutate over this Em9-Am7 chord progression.

Ex. 46

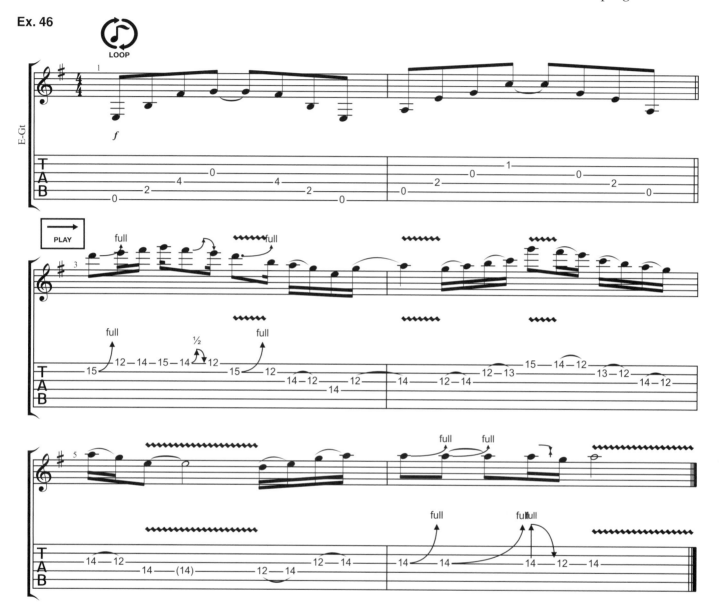

As you play through this example, you should notice the balance applied between the busier phrasing found in the first half, compared to the slower and held melodic phrases in the second half. This type of rhythmic variance between phrases and sections of a solo can help you construct a flowing musical statement, rather than creating a stash of licks pasted together.

It's always best to find a balance in what you're playing and arranging together, and too much of anything is a bad thing – so be sure to mix it up!

Ex.47 reveals where you can perform the root notes of the next chord we're adding to the progression - B7.

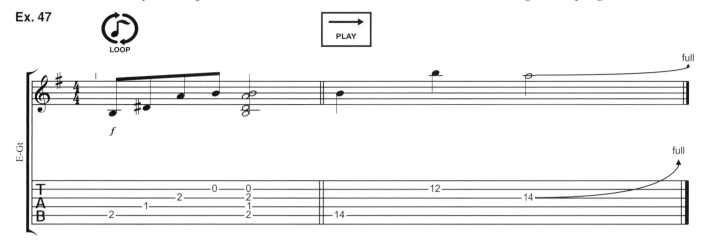

The addition of the B7 chord to this progression creates an interesting and exotic flavor. By adding this chord to the progression, the combination of Em9-Am7-B7 reveals an exotic E Harmonic Minor chord progression and tonality, especially when the chord reaches B7 at the end of the progression, which is showcased in **Ex.48**.

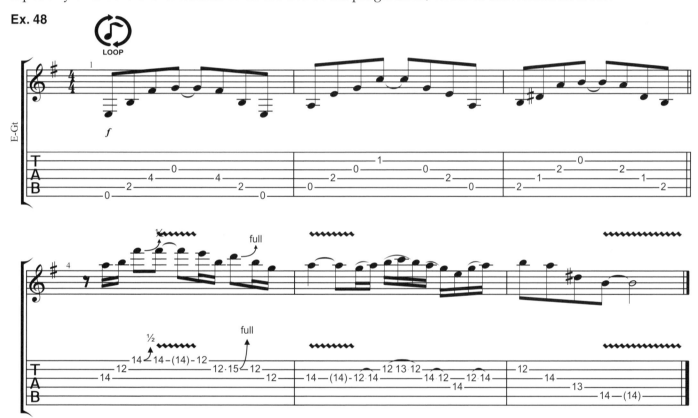

The E Harmonic Minor scale makes an appearance in the third bar of this sample solo over the B7 chord, with the inclusion of the note D#. This exotic scale and sound appears in a number of popular songs within various genres of music, and you can hear this in the music of legendary groups and artists such as Yngwie Malmsteen, The Eagles, and Metallica, not to mention the exotic realms of jazz, flamenco, and Spanish guitar music, with amazing players such as Al Di Meola and Paco De Lucia.

The next example features a targeted four-bar solo that showcases another approach to playing over the B7 chord. **Ex.49** reveals another way to target over this extended chord progression, while staying within a modern rock style.

Ex. 49

In this extended example, notice how the Natural Minor scale is the focus of our phrasing until the final bar, where the E Harmonic Minor scale makes an appearance over the B7 chord. Keeping an alternate scale "up your sleeve" is a common soloing strategy that many guitarists employ. One of the trademarks of a great soloist is the ability to effortlessly weave melodic lines and phrases between different chords, scales, and progressions, and this example gives you a chance to explore this type of phrasing.

Chapter 6 – *Intervals And "The Pentatonic Highway"*

The next area to explore includes the study of intervals and their importance with creating music.

In music, an *interval* is a distance between two (or more) notes, and this includes the notes grouped together to construct scales, chords, arpeggios, melodies, and everything else that you hear in music. Intervals are very important to explore and comprehend, as this area of music theory will noticeably improve the way you hear and perceive music.

The study of intervals is useful for ear training and the refinement with hearing specific frequencies and harmonization in music. The following diagram groups each interval into three classifications. These three classes will help you organize intervals according to how they sound when they're performed in music.

Consonant Intervals
Unison
Perfect 4th
Perfect 5th
Octave

Imperfect Intervals
Minor 3rd
Major 3rd
Minor 6th
Major 6th

Dissonant Intervals
Minor 2nd
Major 2nd
Augmented 4th
Minor 7th
Major 7th

The next diagram shows the arrangement of intervals using the starting note 'E.' Be sure to spend a little time becoming familiar with the interval names and terminology shown below.

Intervals From The 'E' Chromatic Scale

E to E = Unison
E to F = Minor 2nd
E to F# = Major 2nd
E to G = Minor 3rd
E to G# = Major 3rd
E to A = Perfect 4th
E to A# = Augmented 4th
E to B = Perfect 5th
E to C = Minor 6th
E to C# = Major 6th
E to D = Minor 7th
E to D# = Major 7th
E to E = Octave

The next example features the starting note 'E,' which will keep everything in the same key we used in the previous chapter. **Ex.50** reveals a descending intervallic comparison, which will help you hear how this sequence of intervals sound when arranged and played against the Em9 chord. Notice how different each phrase sounds, simply by changing the second note of each two-note sequence.

Ex. 50

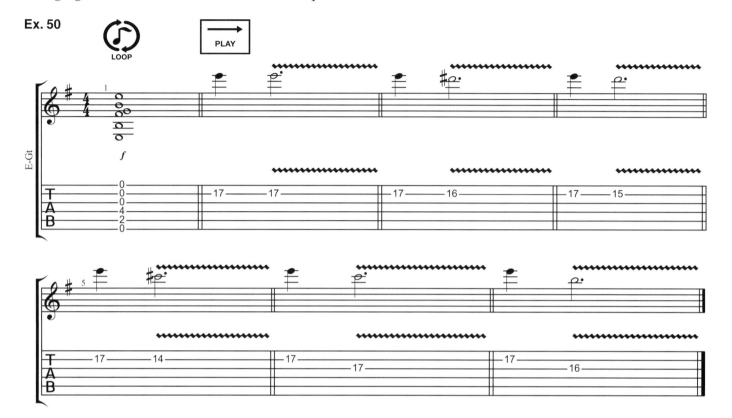

As you play through this example, pay close attention to how each interval sounds individually and take your time exploring and listening to the sounds that intervallic ideas like these produce when they're performed. As you can hear, some intervals have a pleasing sound to the ear, while others are dissonant and create more tension. Finding a balance between tension and release is a crucial element and melodic-themed concept found in all styles of music.

Intervals are the gaps and leaps between the individual notes that are performed in music. This can range from a melody sung by a vocalist, a bass guitar riff, a keyboard intro, or an epic guitar solo. The individual distance between the notes you play have a direct impact of how your licks and phrases sound, and it's interesting to notice how modifying a single note can dramatically change a melodic phrase.

Intervallic Target Tone Exercise

The next example features a useful melodic exercise you can use to find variations of your melodic phrases. This exercise will challenge your ears and fingers and will allow you to hear the possibilities available to you as a soloist, simply by changing the final note of a basic lick.

This type of melodic variation and shift of the final note is a useful and popular method for building interesting musical ideas. You can hear these kinds of phrases and ideas coming from masterful guitarists such as David Gilmour, Stevie Ray Vaughan, Jeff Beck, Eric Clapton, and countless others.

Ex.51 will show you a lot about the importance of note selection when building melodic phrases in music. Pay attention to how different each phrase sounds simply by changing the final note in this melodic exercise.

Ex. 51

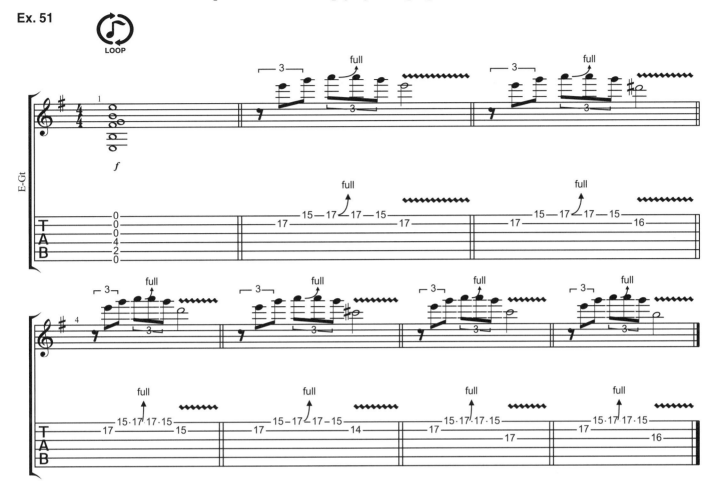

"The Pentatonic Highway"

The final section of this book will uncover a useful and popular method for changing positions on the fretboard and combines several Pentatonic positions as you ascend or descend along the neck. To help you see these movements clearly, examine the fretboard diagram shown below for a "roadmap" of how we're going to connect the neck.

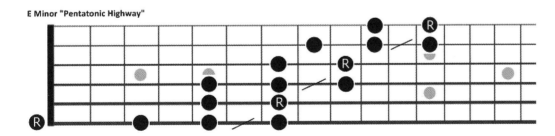

E Minor "Pentatonic Highway"

Notice the finger-friendly movement along the fretboard as this idea uses a shift-slide between the notes 'A' and 'B' within each octave. This helps create a comfortable pattern of notes as this shifted scale pattern moves along the strings and across the neck, and it's recommended to use an index-third fingering combination.

Ex.52 features traveling upward along the neck, and notice that we're using the same positional shift for the slides as this idea moves up the neck and across the strings.

Ex. 52

Spend some time playing through this shape-shifting version of the scale until the fingering and shifting movements become comfortable and fluid. When you have the ascending version of this idea under your fingers, reverse the pattern and practice the descending variation, as demonstrated in **Ex.53**.

Ex. 53

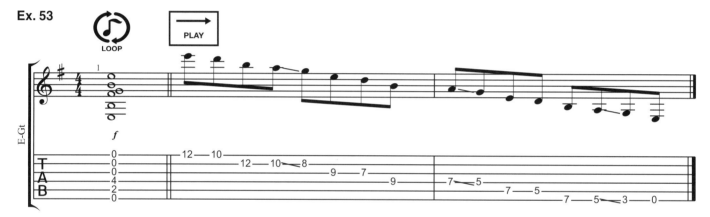

As soon as you're comfortable performing the "Pentatonic Highway" ascending and descending, you can begin creating all kinds of new phrases, licks, and ideas using this popular Pentatonic fretboard concept. The manner in which the scale fingering and notes from the scale line-up, it's worthwhile practice to discover the various ways you can move around the fretboard using this useful idea.

The first solo that uses the "highway" concept is found in **Ex.54**, which will give your fingers a solid descending melodic workout. Take your time and play through this example slowly until the fingering shifts and movements become comfortable and fluid.

Ex. 54

The final example will help you see how to play through a four-bar solo using a series of ascending fretboard movements and shifts. Play through **Ex.55** slowly until the movements and shifts are comfortable, and then this type of phrasing will start flowing under your fingers.

Ex. 55

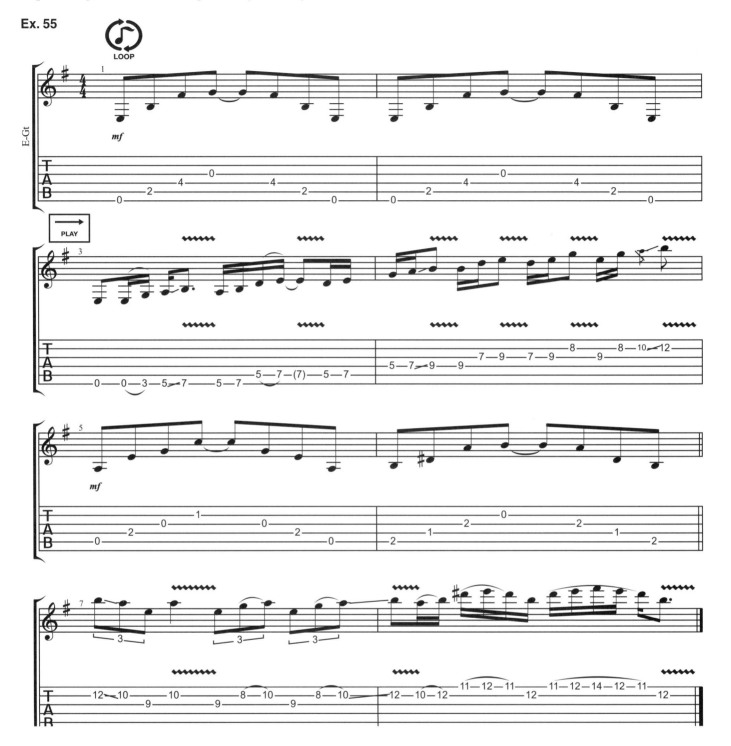

Chapter 7 - *A Brief History Of Looping In Music*

While many musicians are under the impression that loop technology and loop-based music is a modern trend, looping and layering techniques have been active in music since the mid-1950's. Some of this is attributed to pioneering composer Terry Riley, who began experimenting with layered and multi-track performances in his orchestral music. His experiments inspired the forward-thinking ideas that emerged in other music within a short period of time.

Guitar legend Les Paul, with his custom-made Gibson Les Paul.

Around the same time that Riley began experimenting, guitar icon Les Paul designed the Gibson "Les Paul-verizer" guitar, a unique custom instrument that added the controls of an analog dual-head recording unit to his guitar. This interesting concept allowed Les a method of playing, looping, and controlling multiple layered and recorded parts in real-time, which he could access and control either onstage or in the studio.

It's well-documented that Les Paul paved the way for other guitarists to begin live looping and layered performance for guitarists, as numerous musicians were directly inspired by his layering and looping methods in the decades that followed. This includes a wide-range of players and musicians, including loop legends such as Robert Fripp, Brian Eno, Adrian Belew, Bill Frisell, and David Torn, to name a few.

Close-up of the "Les Paul-verizer" Gibson guitar.

Progressive rock guitar legend Robert Fripp (of King Crimson fame) is well-known for the use of his classic "Frippertronics" looping/layering machine, which he created and began using during the 1970's. Fripp's intellectual manner and groundbreaking music created even more of a stir when news spread that he was using a modern form of Les Paul's layering/looping machine. Word of Fripp's musical experiments using this device spread quickly, and everyone took notice of his abstract and experimental musical direction using his unique creation.

Robert Fripp improvising while sitting in front of his "Frippertronics" looping/layering machine.

Fripp's secret-weapon allowed him to loop and layer rhythms and phrases on the fly, where he could continue adding additional drones, harmonies, and textures, creating a combination of multiple guitar parts and looped phrases that swirled around him. Without a doubt, Fripp led the way toward future technical advancement and additional interest in looping technology and layered live performance.

"A way for one person to make an awful lot of noise. Wonderful!" - Robert Fripp

---

Enter the 1980's, and a number of guitarists were found using long-delay settings and time-based layering techniques live and in the studio. This includes legends such as Brian May, David Gilmour, Eddie Van Halen, and The Edge. These artists continued to explore the realm of time-based effects and layers, while simultaneously passing the torch to future generations of players, in turn creating new ideas and applications for using long delay settings and loop-based technology in music.

Guitar legend Chet Atkins won a Grammy Award for the looped performance of his song 'Jam Man' in 1996, a feat that further documented the movement toward creating and writing looped and layered music. In the years that followed, there were a vast array of looping pedals and devices that were released, including classic loop-based models like the Boomerang and the RC-20 from Boss.

In the modern age, you'll find numerous artists that are loop savvy and have embraced creating and performing music using loop-based technology. Modern musicians such as Trey Anastasio, Reggie Watts, KT Tunstall, and Andrew Bird harness loop pedals and gadgets, and have found plenty of new avenues for their music to grow, one looped layer at a time.

Pedal manufacturers have designed various delays, samplers, and loop-minded effect units, giving modern musicians access to loop-based effects in their rig and practice sessions. Although there are a wide-range of looping products available to modern musicians, many of the products on the market have several of the same features, options, and settings. Generally speaking, a simple loop pedal can be purchased for under $100, and this low price-point makes acquiring one of these units attainable and affordable for any musician interested in harnessing this useful and inspiring technology.

One company that's pushing loop technology and design further are the tone and effect gurus at TC Electronic. This includes their innovative and award-winning line of Ditto Looper pedals. While a loop pedal from any manufacturer will suffice, the Ditto Looper is a simple and easy-to-control pedal. Compare the small learning curve of this pedal to some of the more complicated and feature-laden pedals on the market, and you'll understand why this pedal is popular and comes highly recommended.

TC Electronic Ditto Looper

TC Electronic X2 Ditto Looper

The tap-and-go features and ease of use that the Ditto Looper has, makes this unit the recommended pedal for use with the Target Tones method.

The visual diagram below will help you understand how to use the simple one-button/one-knob layout of the Ditto Looper. Press the button once to record, and when you're ready to begin the loop, press the button again to start playing the loop you've created.

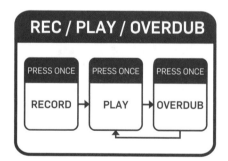
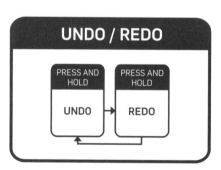
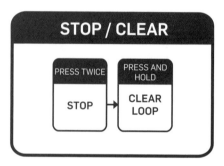

When you're ready to make corrections or edits (example - you want to undo something that you've looped or layered), simply press and hold the button. Press the button twice to stop the loop or press the button twice and hold to clear everything you've created. Once you've erased everything, you can start again and repeat the entire looping process.

This basic diagram and overall function of the Ditto Looper shown above is very similar to every loop pedal or device on the market, as this tap-and-go functionality is the standard of using a loop pedal or audio sampling device. The timing of hitting the button at just the right moment rhythmically is essential for making looped rhythms and backings in-time and suitable to play over.

As with anything, practice makes perfect – good luck!

More Great Books from David Brewster...

ASAP GUITARIST GUIDE
TO STRING BENDING &
VIBRATO

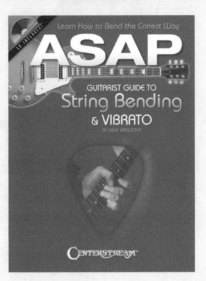

00001347...$19.99

MUTING THE GUITAR

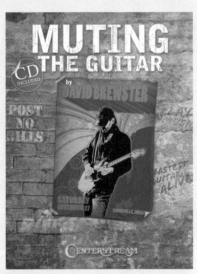

00001199.............................$19.99

GUITAR HARMONY

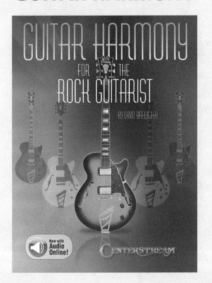

00233915...$19.99

P.O. Box 17878 - Anaheim Hills, CA 92817
(714) 779-9390   www.centerstream-usa.com

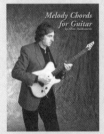

More Great Guitar Books from Centerstream...